Leadership is a critical aspect of success in any organization or endeavor. It involves guiding, motivating, and inspiring others to achieve common goals and objectives.

While some individuals may possess natural leadership abilities, anyone can learn how to become an effective leader with the right tools and strategies.

This book provides the guidance you need to develop your leadership style. Whether you are just starting in a leadership role or are a seasoned professional looking to enhance your skills, this guide will offer valuable insights and practical advice to help you become a more effective leader.

In the first part of this book, we will explore the definition of leadership and the importance of developing a leadership style. We will discuss why having a leadership style is critical to success and how it can help you build stronger relationships with your team members, achieve your goals, and inspire others to do their best work.

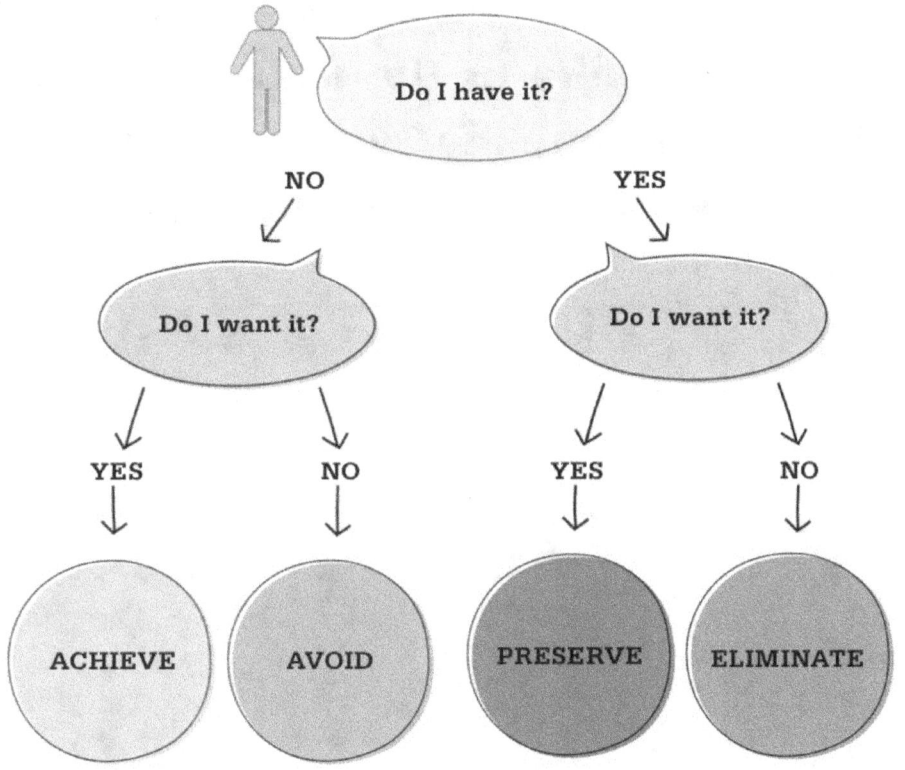

Then, we will dive into specific strategies that you can use to develop your leadership style. From self-assessment tools to seeking feedback from others, effective communication skills to modeling the behavior you want to see, and investing in your personal development, this book will provide you with a comprehensive guide to becoming the best leader you can be.

So, if you are ready to take your leadership skills to the next level, let's get started on the journey towards developing your own unique leadership style.

Introduction

- **Definition of leadership**
- **Overview of the importance of developing a leadership style**

Leadership is a term that is often used but only sometimes well understood. Leadership involves taking responsibility and initiative, inspiring and guiding others, and achieving a shared vision or goal. While leadership is often associated with formal positions of authority, it is also a skill that can be developed by anyone willing to put in the effort.

In this section, we will explore the meaning of leadership and the importance of developing a leadership style. We will start by defining what leadership is and what it entails. We will then discuss why creating a leadership style is essential for individuals in positions of authority and those who want to become leaders.

Leadership Defined

Leadership is the ability to guide and motivate others towards a shared goal or vision. It involves inspiring and influencing people to achieve common objectives, even facing challenges and obstacles. Leadership is not about giving orders or micromanaging but empowering people to take ownership of their work and contribute to the team's success.

A key aspect of leadership is having a clear sense of purpose or vision. This involves knowing what you want to achieve and planning how to get there. It also means communicating your vision clearly and effectively so that others can understand and get behind it.

The Importance of Developing a Leadership Style

Developing a leadership style is important for several reasons. First, it allows you to establish your unique approach to leadership that is authentic and effective. This can help you build credibility and trust with your team members, which is essential for achieving shared goals.

Second, having a leadership style enables you to adapt to different situations and contexts. Different situations may require different approaches to leadership, and having a flexible style can help you navigate these challenges and make the best decisions for your team.

Finally, developing a leadership style can help you achieve personal and professional growth. By reflecting on your strengths and weaknesses, and seeking feedback from others, you can identify areas where you can improve and develop new skills and competencies.

Leadership is an essential skill that can be developed by anyone willing to put in the effort. By defining what leadership means and understanding the importance of developing a leadership style, you can become more effective. In the following sections, we will explore specific strategies and techniques for developing your leadership style so that you can achieve your goals and inspire others to do the same.

Identify Your Strengths and Weaknesses

- Self-assessment tools
- Seeking feedback from others
- Importance of identifying strengths and weaknesses

To become an effective leader, it is important first to understand your strengths and weaknesses. By knowing where you excel and where you may struggle, you can begin to develop strategies for improving your leadership abilities.

Self-assessment tools

One way to identify your strengths and weaknesses is to use self-assessment tools. These tools can help you better understand your personality traits, skills, and areas of expertise. Many types of self-assessment tools are available, including personality tests, career assessments, and skills assessments. By taking these tests and reviewing the results, you can better understand your strengths and weaknesses. My personal favorite is the CliftonStrengths assessment.

Here's a self-assessment tool that you can use to identify you leadership style:

- On a scale of 1 to 5, how confident are you in your current leadership abilities?

- How would you describe your current leadership style? (e.g. authoritative, democratic, laissez-faire, servant, etc.)

- How do you approach decision-making as a leader? (e.g. consensus- building, delegating, analyzing data, intuition, etc.)

- How do you handle conflict resolution among team members?

- How do you provide feedback and coaching to your team members?

- How do you balance being assertive with being empathetic as a leader?

- How do you prioritize tasks and manage your time effectively as a leader? How do you stay up-to-date on new leadership trends and best practices? What are some areas where you feel you could improve your leadership skills?

- What steps will you take to continue developing your leadership style after reading this book?

Seeking feedback from others

Seeking feedback from others is another way to identify your strengths and weaknesses. This can be a challenging step for some people, as it requires a willingness to receive constructive criticism. However, it is important to remember that feedback can be incredibly valuable in helping you identify improvement areas. Consider asking colleagues, supervisors, friends, and family members for feedback on your leadership abilities. Be open to hearing their honest opinions and use their feedback to make positive changes.

Importance of identifying strengths and weaknesses

Identifying your strengths and weaknesses is critical to developing your leadership style. Knowing where you excel allows you to leverage those strengths to become an even more effective leader. For example, if you are a great communicator, you can use that skill to build relationships with team members and inspire others to work towards a common goal. On the other hand, by knowing where you may struggle, you can develop strategies for improving in those areas. For example, if you struggle with time management, you can work on prioritizing tasks and delegating responsibilities to manage your workload better.

Identifying your strengths and weaknesses is an important first step in developing your leadership style. By using self-assessment tools and seeking feedback from others, you can better understand your abilities and develop strategies for becoming a more effective leader. Remember that leadership is an ongoing process, and by continuously evaluating your strengths and weaknesses, you can continue to grow and improve as a leader.

Here is an assessment that can be used for others to evaluate your leadership style:

- On a scale of 1 to 5, how would you rate the leader's ability to communicate effectively with the team?

- On a scale of 1 to 5, how would you rate the leader's ability to provide clear direction and set expectations?

- On a scale of 1 to 5, how would you rate the leader's ability to motivate and inspire the team?

- On a scale of 1 to 5, how would you rate the leader's ability to listen to and consider the opinions of team members?

- On a scale of 1 to 5, how would you rate the leader's ability to make fair and unbiased decisions?

- On a scale of 1 to 5, how would you rate the leader's ability to manage conflict and handle difficult situations?

- On a scale of 1 to 5, how would you rate the leader's ability to delegate tasks and responsibilities effectively?

- On a scale of 1 to 5, how would you rate the leader's ability to hold team members accountable and provide constructive feedback?

- On a scale of 1 to 5, how would you rate the leader's ability to promote teamwork and collaboration?

- What specific strengths or areas for improvement do you see in the leader's leadership style?

Develop Your Communication Skills

- **Effective listening**
- **Understanding different communication styles**
- **Understanding the power of body language**
- **Importance of communication skills in leadership**

Communication is a critical component of effective leadership. A leader who can communicate effectively can inspire and motivate their team to achieve great things. In this section, we will discuss three key aspects of developing your communication skills:

- effective listening,
- understanding different communication styles, and
- understanding the power of body language.

Eective Listening

Effective listening is one of the most important communication skills for a leader to develop. When you listen actively to your team members, you value their input and ideas. Additionally, active listening allows you to gather important information and insights to help you make better decisions. To become an effective listener, focus on being present in the conversation, asking open-ended questions, and providing feedback to show that you understand what is being said.

Understanding Different Communication Styles

Every individual has their own communication style and should be able to adapt it to communicate with others effectively. For example, some people prefer direct communication, while others prefer a more indirect approach. Some people prefer to communicate through written communication, while others prefer face-to-face conversations.

By understanding these different communication styles, you can adjust your communication approach to better connect with your team members and achieve better outcomes.

Understanding the Power of Body Language

Body language is a nonverbal form of communication that can convey much information. As a leader, it is crucial to be aware of your body language and the body language of others. For example, crossed arms and a closed posture can indicate defensiveness or discomfort, while open and relaxed body language can indicate trust and receptiveness.

Additionally, understanding the power of body language can help you to understand the emotions and intentions of others better, even when they are not explicitly stated.

"No matter what people tell you, words and ideas can change the world."
— Robin Williams

Importance of Communication Skills in Leadership

Effective communication is a critical component of successful leadership. When you communicate effectively with your team, you build trust and inspire motivation. Effective communication helps clarify goals and expectations, resolves conflicts, and promotes a positive work environment. By developing your communication skills, you can become a more effective leader and achieve better outcomes for your team.

Developing communication skills is a crucial aspect of becoming an effective leader. By focusing on effective listening, understanding different communication styles, and understanding the power of body language, you can become a more effective communicator and inspire your team to achieve great things. Remember, effective communication is a continuous process, and by consistently working to improve your communication skills, you can continue to grow and develop as a leader.

Success
and
Beyond

Establish Your Credibility

- Building trust with others
- Showing respect to others
- Taking responsibility for actions
  Importance of credibility in leadership

To become an effective leader, it is essential to establish credibility with your team. Credibility is trust and respect, built over time through consistent actions and behaviors. This section will explore three key strategies for establishing your credibility as a leader: building trust with others, showing respect to others, and taking responsibility for your actions.

Building Trust with Others

Trust is a foundational element of any successful relationship, including the relationship between a leader and their team. When team members trust their leader, they are more likely to feel motivated, engaged, and committed to the organization's goals. To build trust with your team, it is important to be transparent, honest, and consistent in your actions and communication. Additionally, follow through on your commitments, be willing to admit mistakes, and make amends when necessary.

Showing Respect to Others

Respect is another essential component of building credibility as a leader. When you show respect to others, you demonstrate that you value their contributions and perspectives and create an environment of mutual trust and support. To show respect to your team members, listen actively, seek out their opinions and ideas, and acknowledge their strengths and accomplishments. Additionally, avoid demeaning or dismissive language, and be mindful of nonverbal cues that could indicate disrespect.

Taking Responsibility for Your Actions

Leadership requires a willingness to take responsibility for one's actions and decisions. When you accept responsibility for your mistakes, you demonstrate accountability and integrity and build credibility with your team. Take responsibility for your actions, be willing to own your error, and take steps to rectify the situation. Additionally, be willing to accept feedback and criticism and be open to making changes when necessary.

Importance of Credibility in Leadership

Credibility is essential for effective leadership, as it creates an environment of trust and respect that enables team members to work together towards shared goals. Establishing credibility with your team creates a culture of accountability, transparency, and mutual support that can lead to improved performance and outcomes. Additionally, credible leaders are more likely to inspire their team members, build strong relationships with stakeholders, and create a positive reputation for their organization.

Establishing your credibility as a leader is a critical component of effective leadership. You can become an incredible leader by building trust with others, showing respect to others, and taking responsibility for your actions. Credibility is built over time through consistent actions and behaviors, requiring ongoing effort and attention. By establishing your credibility as a leader, you can create a foundation for success that will benefit you and your team.

Model the Behavior You Want to See

- Leading by example
- Setting clear expectations for others
- Holding yourself and others accountable
- Importance of modeling behavior in leadership

As a leader, your behavior sets the tone for your team. When you model the behavior you want to see in others, you create a culture of excellence, accountability, and high performance. In this section, we will explore three key strategies for modeling behavior as a leader: leading by example, setting clear expectations for others, and holding yourself and others accountable.

Leading by Example

Leading by example is one of the most powerful ways to model behavior as a leader. When you demonstrate the behaviors and values you want your team to emulate, you create a culture of excellence and inspire your team members to do their best. To lead by example, practice what you preach, show a strong work ethic and be willing to get your hands dirty when necessary.

Setting Clear Expectations for Others

In addition to leading by example, setting clear expectations for your team members is essential. When everyone knows what is expected of them, it is easier to hold people accountable and ensure everyone is working towards the same goals. To set clear expectations, communicate your goals and priorities, establish performance metrics, and provide regular feedback and coaching.

THERE IS NO HACK.
THERE IS NO SHORTCUT.
THERE IS NO EASY WAY.

Holding Yourself and Others Accountable

As a leader, holding yourself and others accountable for achieving results is essential. When you hold yourself accountable, you demonstrate integrity and are committed to achieving your goals. When you hold others accountable, you create a high-performance culture and ensure that everyone does their part to contribute to the organization's success. To hold yourself and others accountable, establish clear performance metrics, provide regular feedback, and hold team members responsible for their actions and decisions.

Importance of Modeling Behavior in Leadership

Modeling behavior is critical to effective leadership, as it creates a culture of excellence, accountability, and high performance. When you lead by example, set clear expectations for others, and hold yourself and others accountable, you create a foundation for success that can drive improved outcomes and results. Additionally, modeling behavior can inspire your team members, build trust and respect, and help you achieve your goals more effectively.

Another benefit of modeling behavior is that it helps leaders identify improvement areas. When leaders know their strengths and weaknesses, they can model the behavior they want to see in others while working on their development. This shows humility and a willingness to learn, which can inspire others to do the same.

Modeling behavior is a key strategy for effective leadership. Leading by example, setting clear expectations, and holding yourself and others accountable can create a culture of excellence and inspire your team members to do their best work. Remember, modeling behavior requires ongoing effort and attention, and it is essential to stay committed to your goals and values to achieve success. By focusing on modeling behavior, you can create a strong foundation for success that will benefit both you and your team.

Invest in Your Personal Development

- **Seeking out mentors**
- **Taking advantage of training opportunities**
- **Reading books and articles on leadership**
- **Importance of personal development in leadership**

As a leader, your personal development is critical to your success. The more you invest in your growth and development, the more effective you will be in your role. In this section, we will explore three key strategies for investing in your personal development:

- seeking out mentors,
- taking advantage of training opportunities, and
- reading books and articles on leadership.

Seeking Out Mentors

One of the most valuable resources for personal development is a mentor. A mentor can provide guidance, support, and advice based on their experiences and expertise. To find a mentor, look for someone in your industry or field who has achieved success and has a leadership style you admire. Reach out to them and ask if they would be willing to mentor you and be prepared to invest time and effort in building the relationship.

Taking Advantage of Training Opportunities

Another way to invest in personal development is to take advantage of training opportunities. This can include attending conferences, workshops, and seminars and participating in online courses and webinars. Look for opportunities that align with your goals and interests, and apply what you learn in your work.

Reading Books and Articles on Leadership

Reading books and articles on leadership is a powerful way to invest in personal development. Countless resources are available on various topics, from communication skills to team management to strategy development. Look for books and articles that align with your interests and goals, and apply what you learn in your leadership role.

Success and Beyond Presents:
How to Develop Your Leadership Style

James D. Washington, DBA

Importance of Personal Development in Leadership

Investing in your personal development is critical to your success as a leader. It can help you improve your skills, expand your knowledge, and stay current with trends and best practices in your industry. Personal development can also help you stay motivated and engaged in your work as you learn and grow. By investing in your personal development, you are not only improving yourself but also setting an example for your team members to follow.

Investing in your personal development is essential to your success as a leader. By seeking out mentors, taking advantage of training opportunities, and reading books and articles on leadership, and you can improve your skills, expand your knowledge, and stay current with trends and best practices in your industry.

Personal development requires ongoing effort and commitment, but the rewards are worth the investment. Investing in yourself can make you a more effective and successful leader and inspire your team members to do the same.

Conclusion

- Recap of the importance of developing a leadership style
- Encouragement to take the steps to develop your own style

In this eBook, we have explored the key strategies for developing your leadership style. We have discussed the importance of identifying your strengths and weaknesses, developing your communication skills, establishing your credibility, modeling the behavior you want to see, and investing in your personal development.

Leadership is not a one-size-fits-all approach. Every leader has their own unique style, based on their strengths, experiences, and values. However, by following the strategies outlined in this book, you can develop your own effective leadership style that will help you achieve your goals and inspire your team members.

It is important to remember that developing your leadership style is an ongoing process. It requires self-reflection, practice, and a willingness to learn and grow. But the benefits of investing in your leadership development are significant. You can become a more effective communicator, build stronger relationships with your team members, and achieve greater success in your role.

So, I encourage you to take the steps to develop your own leadership style. Use the strategies outlined in this book as a starting point, but also be open to exploring new approaches and learning from your experiences. Remember, leadership is not about being perfect, but about continually improving and growing as a leader.

Thank you for reading this book on how to develop your leadership style. I wish you the best of luck on your leadership journey.

About the Author

Dr. Washington is a Certified Gallup Strength Coach who believes that success is not just reserved for the lucky few, but it's attainable for anyone who's willing to put in the work. With years of experience in helping individuals and organizations unlock their full potential, Dr. Washington has developed a reputation for delivering results that go beyond expectations.

As a firm believer in the power of personal strengths, Dr. Washington works closely with clients to identify their unique talents and develop a customized plan to help them achieve their goals. With his warm and engaging personality, he creates a safe space where clients can share their fears and doubts, while providing them with the tools and support they need to overcome any obstacle.

If you're ready to take your life to the next level, then follow Success and Beyond and begin your journey to success today! With Dr. Washington as your guide, you'll discover that success is not just a destination, but a journey filled with exciting challenges and endless possibilities.